YOUR Amazing BRAIN

THE EPIC ILLUSTRATED GUIDE

For Dr. Jonathan Baylin,
Thank you for sharing your
amazing brain with me.

For the adults reading this:

Brains are complicated! There is a lot of information packed into this book. Take your time exploring. Read different sections on different days. Have a short conversation and come back to the topic another time. See page 37 for more tips. Above all, let curiosity and connection be your guide.

Here is a suggested path to help you navigate:

Duplication and Copyright

NATIONAL CENTER for
YOUTH ISSUES

P.O. Box 22185
Chattanooga, TN 37422-2185
423.899.5714 • 866.318.6294
fax: 423.899.4547 • www.ncyi.org

ISBN: 9781931636506
E-BOOK ISBN: 9781931636513
© 2023 National Center for Youth Issues, Chattanooga, TN
All rights reserved.
Written by: Jessica Sinarski
Published by National Center for Youth Issues
Printed in the U.S.A. • August 2023

Cataloging-in-Publication Data has been applied for and may be obtained from the Library of Congress.

Third party links are accurate at the time of publication, but may change over time.

NCYI titles may be purchased in bulk at special discounts for educational, business, fundraising, or promotional use. For more information, please email sales@ncyi.org.

A CLOSER LOOK

You might have seen pictures of the brain that look like a lumpy, pink blob.

But if you look a little closer, you'll see a moving masterpiece of chemicals, electricity, and **tiny little working parts called CELLS.**

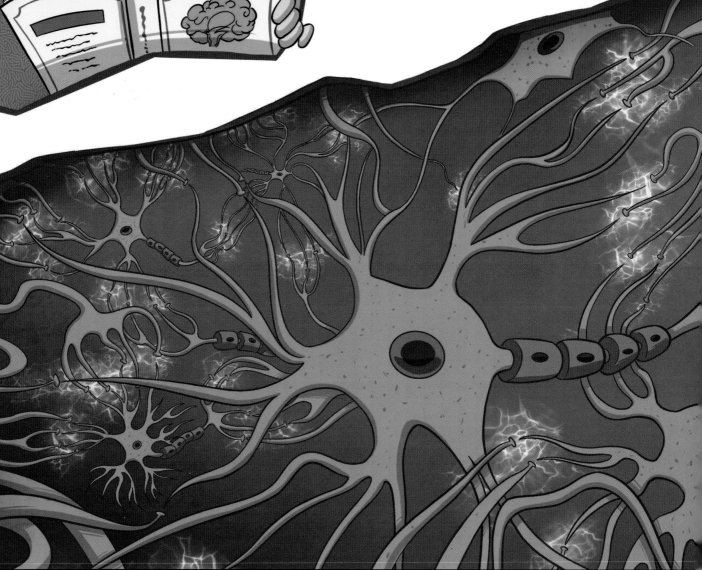

If you look *really* close, you will see over 85 billion of these funny-looking things called neurons. **NEURONS are the brain cells that send and receive messages.**

Get to Know a Neuron!

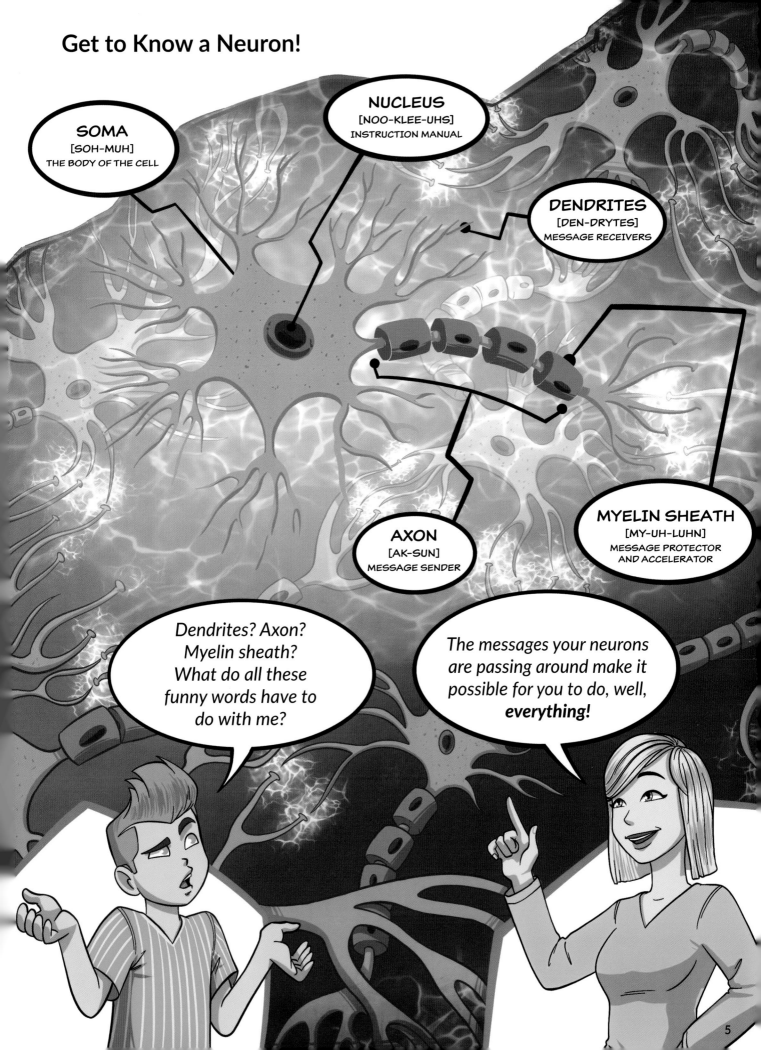

BRAIN CELLS IN ACTION

Brain cells team up to get stuff done. They connect across long distances like the most complicated game of telephone you can imagine!

Here's how it works...

1. Dendrites listen for a message, a **little package of chemicals called NEUROTRANSMITTERS**.

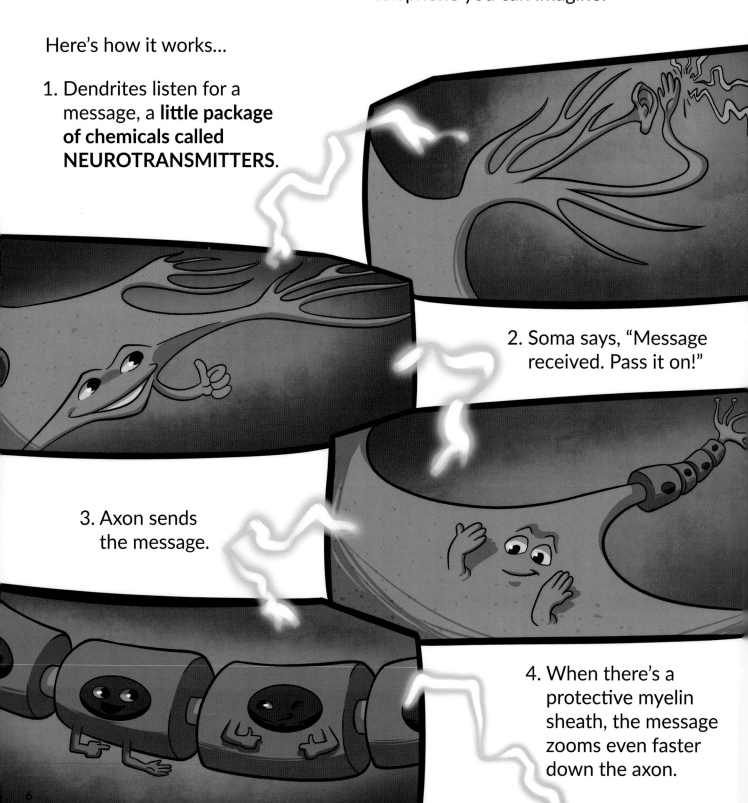

2. Soma says, "Message received. Pass it on!"

3. Axon sends the message.

4. When there's a protective myelin sheath, the message zooms even faster down the axon.

5. Then, electricity pushes the message into the **SYNAPSE**—**that little space between two neurons,** for the next listening dendrites.

6. This cycle repeats about a gazillion times with little messages flying from neuron to neuron all over your brain and out into your body.

But wait! There's more!

GLIAL [GLEE-uhl] **CELLS are the other main type of brain cell.** They do a *lot* to keep the brain running smoothly! "Glia" [GLEE-uh] comes from the Greek word for glue because one of their jobs is to hold neurons in place. They wrap around axons to speed things along, like insulation on a wire. Glia also bring food and oxygen to neurons and even clean up after them. Fun fact: Humans have about 10 times as many glial cells as neurons.

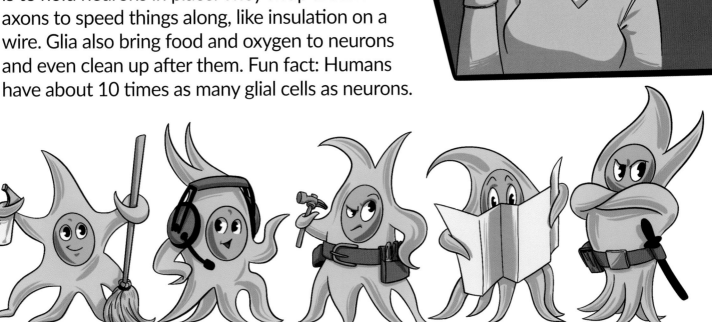

YOUR NERVOUS SYSTEM

Your brain doesn't work alone. **The network of connections between your body and brain is called the NERVOUS SYSTEM...** not because it's scared, but because it is made up of nerves.

NERVES are groups of neurons that send information from your brain to your body and back to the brain.

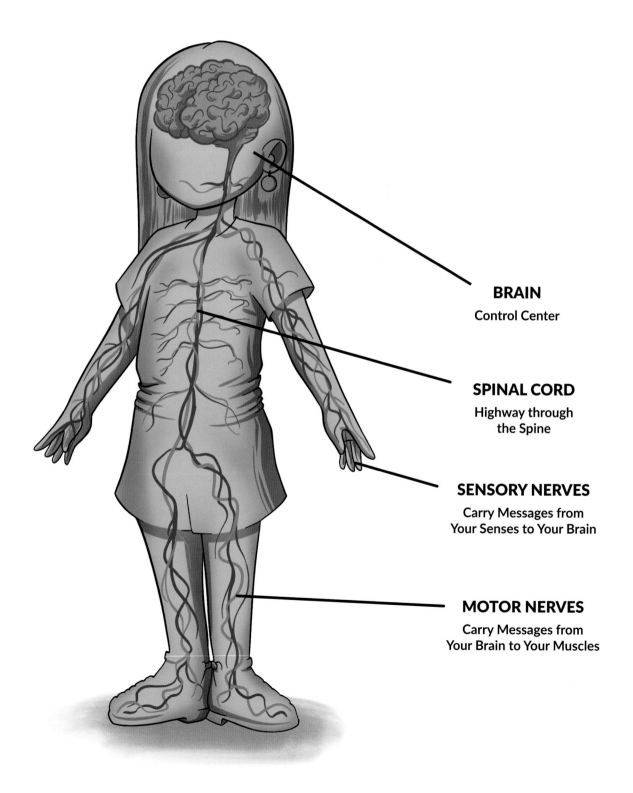

BRAIN

Control Center

SPINAL CORD

Highway through
the Spine

SENSORY NERVES

Carry Messages from
Your Senses to Your Brain

MOTOR NERVES

Carry Messages from
Your Brain to Your Muscles

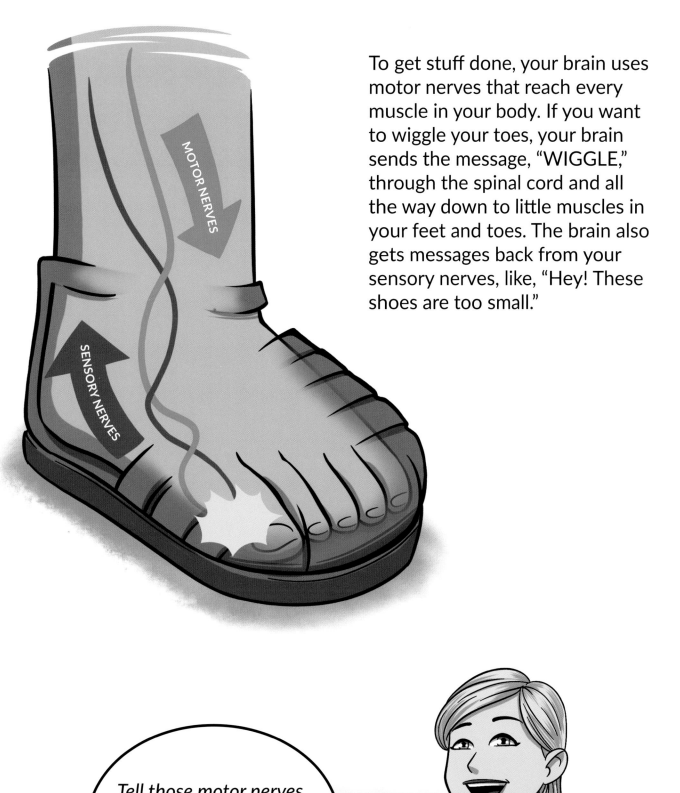

To get stuff done, your brain uses motor nerves that reach every muscle in your body. If you want to wiggle your toes, your brain sends the message, "WIGGLE," through the spinal cord and all the way down to little muscles in your feet and toes. The brain also gets messages back from your sensory nerves, like, "Hey! These shoes are too small."

Tell those motor nerves in your arm and hand to flip the page so you can learn more!

YOUR *EiGHT* SENSES

Your brain gets LOTS of messages from your senses: about 11 million tiny packages of electrical and chemical information *every second!* To begin to understand how you can be the boss of your brain, let's get to know all eight of your sensational senses.

Your five main senses tell you what's happening *outside* your body.

| SIGHT | HEARING | TOUCH | SMELL | TASTE |

You also have three hidden (but super important) senses *inside*.

VESTIBULAR

[veh-STI-byuh-luhr]

movement and balance

These neurons in your inner ear give your brain little details to help you feel stable and anchored. Lots of crawling, swinging, climbing, hanging upside-down, biking or scooting, spinning, and other movements feed this important sense.

PROPRIOCEPTION

[pro-pree-oh-SEP-shun]

pressure, impact, and weight

Without the sensory neurons that connect to your muscles and joints, you would feel like you're floating away in outer space! Pushing, pulling, jumping, clapping, drumming, walking, running, carrying something heavy, and even chewing gum can help your body feel like it's grounded here on planet earth.

INTEROCEPTION

[in-tuhr-oh-SEP-shun]

inner world

The sensory neurons from your internal organs and skin share important information with your brain all day long. Whenever you take a deep breath or pause and think things through, you are strengthening this inner sense!

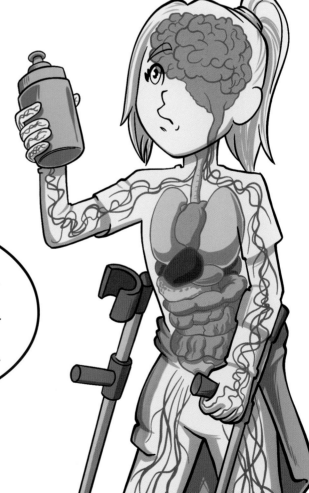

An INTERNAL ORGAN is a part of your body under the skin that performs a specific function, like your lungs taking in oxygen or your heart pumping blood.

INFORMATION OVERLOAD

It's easy to see how the game of telephone that your 86 billion neurons are playing can get complicated.

OUTSIDE

INSIDE

Your five main senses send messages about what is going on *outside* your body.

Your three hidden senses concentrate on what's happening *inside* at all times.

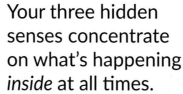

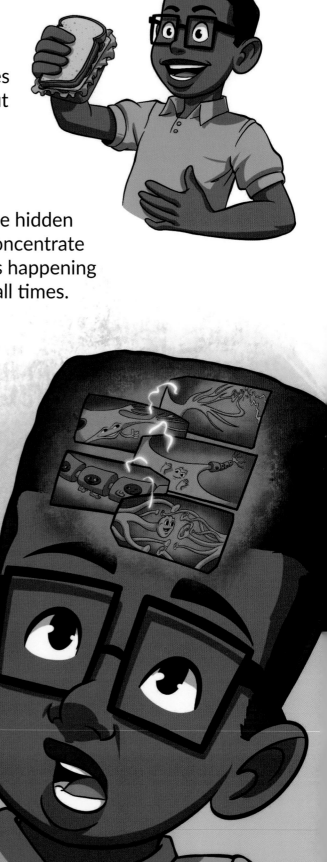

Plus, your brain is always wondering about what is going on *between* you and the people around you...sometimes without you even realizing it!

What is their face telling you?
What does their tone of voice mean?
What is their body saying?

13

YOUR BRAIN HAS STAIRS[1]

Okay, your brain doesn't *actually* have stairs, but when you are born, your brain is a lot like a two-story house that is under construction. The neurons in your Downstairs Brain are ready for action, but the Upstairs Brain is still developing for another 25 years!

Upstairs Brain

Cerebral [ser-EE-bruhl] **Cortex**
- **the large, wrinkly outer portion of your brain**
- **lets you connect, play, talk, learn, create, and think things through**

Downstairs Brain

Brain Stem
- **quick responder**
- **in charge of automatic actions like breathing and heartbeat**

Limbic [LIM-bik] **System**
- **feeling and memory center in the middle of your brain**
- **colors sensory messages based on your experiences and emotions**

1. Adapted from *The Whole-Brain Child* by Daniel J. Siegel, MD and Tina Payne Bryson, Ph

You can use your hand to talk about different parts of your brain.

Hold open your hand, fold over your thumb, and make a fist. This is your brain. Your fingers are the Upstairs Brain that is growing and making new connections even as you read this book!

UPSTAIRS BRAIN

Your thumbnail represents a special part of your Downstairs Brain called the **AMYGDALA** [uh-MIG-duh-luh]. **This little almond-shaped group of neurons acts like an alarm system and traffic director.**

Your Amygdala instantly decides if the messages being delivered by your senses are safe enough for your Upstairs Brain to run things, or... DANGER! DANGER! Your Downstairs Brain takes over, acting without thinking. The Amygdala sends in one of your animal superpowers to save the day!

The problem is, the Downstairs Brain can get *extra* protective. Humans have lots of false alarms every day! It takes oodles of practice to strengthen your Upstairs Brain so it can bring its calm, curious, creative solutions to the big feelings coming up from your "Act Without Thinking" team.

X-RAY VISION FOR THE DOWNSTAIRS BRAIN

The brain pays a lot of attention to one big question: **Am I safe?**

At the slightest hint of danger, feeling left out, or even just something you don't like, your Amygdala is ready to send in your Downstairs Brain Protectors.

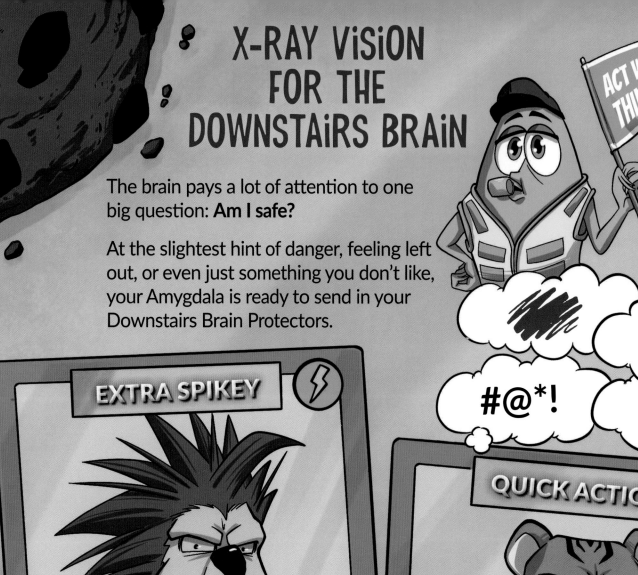

ACT WITHOUT THINKING

#@*!

I hate this!

EXTRA SPIKEY

MOTTO	"I stay grumpy so you don't get hurt!"
POWER	Prickly powers to keep people away
SPECIAL SKILLS	Teams up with other Porcupine Brains to complain and blame

This is the worst.

You don't get it.

I don't want to!

I don't need you.

QUICK ACTION!

MOTTO	"I was born ready to ROAR!"
POWER	LARGE AND IN CHARGE
SPECIAL SKILLS	Does maximum damage!

WHO'S IN CHARGE HERE?

Your brain is a pro at getting stuff done that you don't even notice! It's a good thing, too. If not, you would have to spend all day and night telling your heart to beat, your lungs to breathe, your stomach to digest, your eyes to blink, and on and on and on. That wouldn't leave much time for exploring and having fun.

Act Without Thinking: Protection Mode

1. Sensory nerves in Jeff's fingers send an urgent message up the spinal cord that says, "DANGER! GET AWAY!"

2. Neurons in the brain stem jump to action and immediately send a message back down Jeff's motor nerves to say, "Tiger! ACT FAST! GET AWAY!"

Way to go, Downstairs Brain!

Think Before Acting: Connection Mode

Sensory nerves in Jeff's eyes send neurotransmitters to the brain stem and Amygdala.

The picture isn't very clear yet, but there are no signs of danger, so the Downstairs Brain passes it upstairs for more information.

The cerebral cortex looks more carefully and sees that it's a friend waving.

The message goes back through the limbic system, which says: "Yay! That's my friend. New message for the Upstairs Brain—wave back. Oh, and smile too!"

A special part of the Upstairs Brain called the motor cortex gets the message and sends it on to Jeff's hand and face.

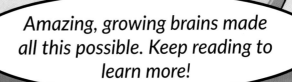

Amazing, growing brains made all this possible. Keep reading to learn more!

BRAINS UNDER CONSTRUCTION

Act Without Thinking

The Downstairs Brain is really focused on keeping you alive. This is where quick reactions and big feelings live.

This team is all about survival.

✓ Heart: Beat
✓ Lungs: Breathe
✓ Mouth: Drink milk
✓ Eyes: Blink

I'm tired!

Ouch! That hurt!

I'm hungry!

I pooped!

I'm cold!

Did you notice there aren't a lot of words coming from this part of the brain? Over time, with a lot of help from safe adults, the Upstairs Brain is built.

Think Before Acting

You use your Upstairs Brain to play, learn, and have fun. It also helps you deal with all the emotions coming from the Downstairs Brain.

This team of neurons is in charge of:

Asking for Help

Go night, night?

Making a Plan

I have to be careful so I don't get hurt.

Solving Problems

I'll get a snack.

Understanding Ourselves

May I please go to the bathroom?

Caring About Others

You look cold. Want to borrow my sweatshirt?

And SO MUCH MORE!

*Psst. Grown-ups, did you know that kids' Downstairs Brain Protectors need lots of help from **your** Upstairs Brain before **their** "think before acting" team grows strong enough to take charge?*

Your Amygdala was born ready to send in your Downstairs Brain Protectors for all kinds of things. Sometimes you need Tiger speed, like when Jeff pulled his hand away from the hot stove. Without some help from the Upstairs Brain, though, every little thing feels dangerous to the Amygdala.

My motto is better-safe-than-sorry.

I see danger EVERYWHERE.

When Byron was worried that the kids at his new school didn't like him, his Amygdala said, "DANGER! You don't want to get left out!" The feeling was really big because he never felt like he fit in anywhere. His Chameleon Brain took over. He tried and tried to get the kids in his class to like him, so much that he ended up not really being himself.

$$4 \times 1000 + 3 \times 20 =$$

Sometimes the danger seems so big that Protectors team up!

It was Jeff's turn to do a math problem on the board, but in his mind, his Amygdala was saying...

"This is confusing. You might fail! This will be suuuuuper embarrassing!!"

He folded his arms across his chest as his Porcupine Brain thought, "Math is stupid!" Then Turtle shut down started as he pulled his hoodie up over his head and hid his face.

And sometimes your Amygdala finds even *more* Protectors to call on.

I might get in trouble?

Danger!

Send in the Squirrel Protector to lie and sneak.

I didn't eat it.

I have to do something I don't want to do? Danger!

It's easy to see how the Downstairs Brain can get us in trouble, but that's not the end of the story. You can be the boss of your brain!

THE ABC'S YOUR UPSTAIRS BRAIN NEEDS

Your brain works best when the messages are flowing smoothly between both teams.
Try this three-step plan to strengthen the staircase of your mind!

It's as simple as A-B-C.

A QUICK PAUSE
BE CURIOUS
CHOOSE WISELY

A kid bumps into you in the hall.

Your Amygdala says, "Danger! Tiger power, activate!"

Your Tiger Protector is pretty sure the kid is a jerk and you should go push her back, but you use your Upstairs Brain to take A QUICK PAUSE.

Your Amygdala says, "Okay, Tiger. Stay alert while I send this message upstairs for more information."

The lights are on in your Upstairs Brain, which helps you BE CURIOUS.

You might see:

- She was going too fast, and it was an accident.
- Her hands were full, and she bumped you as she was dropping her books.
- She has tears in her eyes.

You CHOOSE WISELY how you will respond. Your Upstairs Brain is powered up, and it lets your Amygdala know, "All clear. I'm going to help her out. No Tiger powers needed."

PROTECTiON MODE VS. CONNECTiON MODE

With all the messages coming its way, it is easy for the Amygdala to slide into protection mode. As you strengthen the staircase of your mind, you can choose connection mode more and more by getting your Upstairs Brain involved.

NOT INVITED

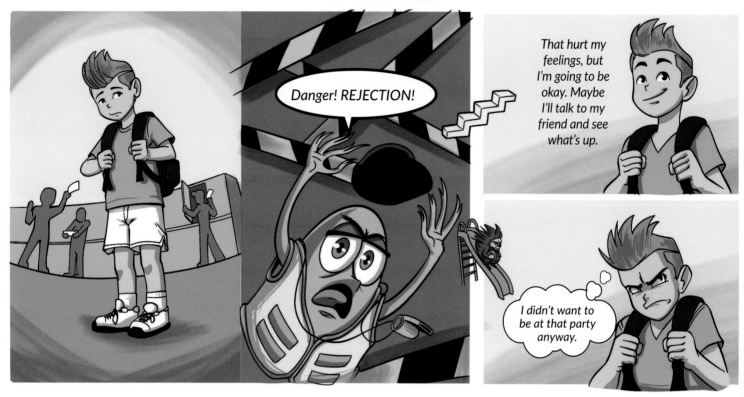

GIVING A PRESENTATION

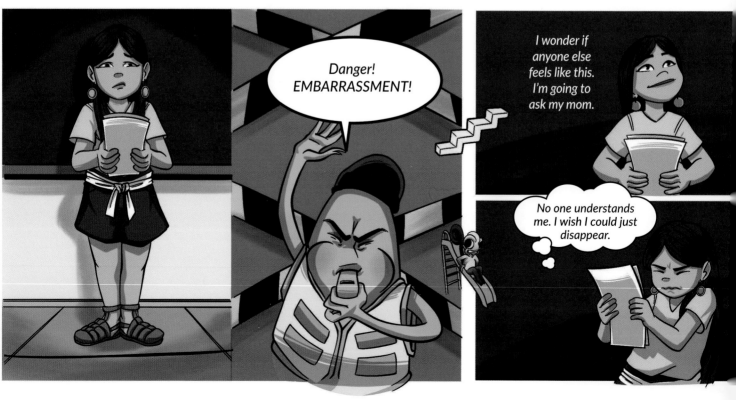

LOSING A GAME

MORE CHORES THAN A SIBLING

PRACTICE MAKES ~~PERFECT~~ BETTER

Most of the things that you do without thinking now took a LOT of practice at first.

Each time you learn a new skill, neurons have to team up.

The more you practice, the stronger the connections get. Think about tying your shoes. In the beginning, your eyes, fingers, and thoughts all had to pay close attention.

- The sensory nerves in your fingers and eyes told your brain where the laces are.
- Your brain sent messages back to squeeze and twist and pull.
- Maybe you made "bunny ears" or thought about each step of looping, crossing, and pulling through.
- Every time you practiced, all those "shoe tying" pathways between your brain and body got a little stronger!

Go slow to go fast. Let those signals get all the way to your Upstairs Brain. When we rush, sometimes we miss things.

Chunk it. Break the problem into smaller parts. Set goals for little chunks of learning, like "I will practice my fours multiplication facts for 10 minutes every night before dinner this week."

When you mess up, try again! Your Amygdala might be yelling, "Danger! Failure!" But mistakes are an essential part of growing your brain! When you take the time to figure out what went wrong, you help your neurons make super-speed pathways to do it better next time.

Practice the tricky part. When something doesn't go as planned, use your ABC's to figure out what the hardest part is. Then your wise choice will be to practice that part over and over. Athletes and musicians do this all the time to master their craft.

Tell yourself the *whole* story. There will be times you get stuck on a hard assignment or feel frustrated as you are learning something new. The word "and" can be quite powerful in those moments. I'm so frustrated, *and* I know I will find my way through.

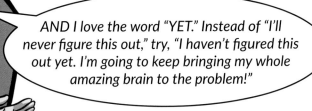

AND I love the word "YET." Instead of "I'll never figure this out," try, "I haven't figured this out yet. I'm going to keep bringing my whole amazing brain to the problem!"

You can do hard things. Every time you look back on how you did something challenging, you strengthen connections in your brain that will help you face the next challenge.

DiD YOU KNOW?

Your brain is always changing! Your brain grows so much in the first three years of life that it has to trim back some connections. Well-used pathways get strengthened with a myelin sheath so that signals can zoom where they need to go. That's what helps you do a LOT more cool stuff now than you could do as a three-year-old!

Your brain produces enough electricity to power a small lightbulb!

Just because something feels good doesn't mean it's good for you. Sometimes our chemical messengers say, "More! More! More!" to stuff like video games, sugary foods, and other things that won't help us feel good in the long run. With practice, you can notice when enough is enough and use your Upstairs Brain to put on the brakes.

Screens and social media are designed to make your brain want MORE! MORE! MORE! It might seem like *everyone* has a phone these days, but the longer you wait, the better it is for your brain!

My older sister said that her Chameleon Brain wants "likes" online, but she always feels better when she just hangs out with her friends instead.

Signals in your brain can travel faster than a race car.

Sharing is caring...sometimes. Emotions are contagious. One person's "Downstairs Brain moment" can set off another and another until it's a mess of Tiger, Turtle, Porcupine, and Chameleon Protectors running the show. That's because your brain is organized to act and feel before you think. When your Amygdala alarm goes off, remember to take A QUICK PAUSE, BE CURIOUS, and CHOOSE WISELY.

Your brain is more powerful than the most advanced supercomputer.

Your brain is 73% water.

Being kind, thinking about how others feel, and noticing the good in others helps you grow important connections in your Upstairs Brain. Try writing a thank-you note or really listening to your grandma's stories the next time you are together. Look for ways to show kindness to others, like smiling and saying hello, helping without being asked, or checking in with a friend who seems a little down.

We need each other! Your brain pays a lot of attention to other people. It has since you were a tiny baby, looking for your safe grown-ups. It's easy for the Amygdala to send you into protection mode, but the more your Upstairs Brain hangs out with other Upstairs Brains, the better it is for everyone!

Brain cells come in all different shapes and sizes. Most are so small you need a microscope to see them, and some are as long as your leg!

TEN MORE BRAIN BOOSTING HABITS

Wondering what else you can do to take good care of your amazing brain?
Practice these healthy habits more and more each day!

1. Connect with Safe Adults.

The human brain takes a LONG time to grow up—over 25 years! In that time (and long after) we need grown-ups we can depend on, who understand our feelings, take care of us, and help us grow.

2. PLAY!

Your brain makes lots of important connections when you play games, use your imagination, or shoot hoops outside. Play can even make chores more fun! Try turning on some music and dancing around as you help clean up after dinner.

3. Eat Some Greens.

A balanced diet with plenty of vegetables, fiber, protein, and healthy fats gives your brain the nutrients it needs to learn and grow.

When I don't have enough to eat, my Porcupine Brain takes over. I can't think straight, and EVERYTHING is annoying.

4. Move Your Body to Fuel Your Brain.

Your brain LOVES movement. Running around and getting sweaty, swinging on the playground, doing a few jumping jacks, and even just stretching your arms over your head can help create the chemical messages (neurotransmitters) that your brain needs.

My teacher always says, "FAIL stands for First Attempt In Learning!"

5. Try New Things.

Get creative! Find interesting ways to use the same old thing, like making a spaceship out of a cardboard box or turning an egg carton into an art project. Try new ways to solve everyday problems, and if it doesn't work...try again!

Hey, Amygdala, I know you're nervous about that big test, but I studied hard and I'm ready!

6. Practice the Pause.

Remember, the first step to getting your Upstairs Brain in charge is A QUICK PAUSE. Take a breath and think about what is going on inside. It might sound silly, but you can talk to different parts of your brain.

7. Become a Feelings Detective.

When you use your Upstairs Brain to say hello to big, uncomfortable feelings, your Amygdala doesn't have to send in the "act without thinking" team. You can say hello to your worry, sadness, or anger, and all the heavy stuff that might be underneath. With some Upstairs Brain help, you can find your way through without hurting yourself or someone else along the way.

8. Get Plenty of Sleep.

Your brain is hard at work when you are sleeping! That's when your glial cells do their cleaning, teams of neurons file away the things you learned that day so you can remember it later, new connections are strengthened, and what's not needed is cleaned up.

9. Notice the Good.

Your brain naturally pays a lot of attention to things that might be dangerous or even just uncomfortable, but you are the boss of your brain! Take some time each day to pay attention to the people, places, and moments that bring you joy. It might be big things like winning an art contest or something simple like how comfy your favorite blanket feels.

I feel better if, on the days I have some screen time, I go for a bike ride too.

10. Choose Green Time Over Screen Time.

Sure, you might use a device from time to time, but the real 3D world is so much better for your brain than getting lost in video games and other entertainment.

EVERY BRAIN IS UNIQUE

The connections in your brain are as unique as your fingerprint. Scientists are learning more and more that there is no such thing as "normal." Maybe learning to read was easy but math has been hard, or talking to friends is no problem but sports aren't your thing. What sets off your Amygdala alarm or calms your Tiger Brain might be different than your friends or family. It's not weird, it's human!

Celebrate your strengths...

Get some help with the tough stuff...

And keep growing your amazing brain!

QUICK GUIDE FOR GROWN-UPS

Brain development is all about CONNECTIONS—inside and out! Kids need connections to safe adults to help their Downstairs and Upstairs Brain connect!

BRAIN DEVELOPMENT BEGINS IN UTERO.

WHEN BABIES ARE BORN, THE DOWNSTAIRS BRAIN IS READY TO GO!

THEY NEED LOTS OF SOOTHING HELP FROM YOUR UPSTAIRS BRAIN.[2]

THIS LETS BABY'S AMYGDALA KNOW THAT IT IS SAFE ENOUGH TO BEGIN CONSTRUCTION UPSTAIRS.

ONE MILLION NEW NEURAL CONNECTIONS DEVELOP PER SECOND IN THOSE EARLY YEARS.[3] PLAY IS AN ESPECIALLY IMPORTANT PART OF BUILDING THE UPSTAIRS BRAIN.

KIDS NEED TO KNOW THEIR CRIES AND SMILES MATTER.

WITHOUT SAFETY, CARE, AND CONNECTION, THE "ACT WITHOUT THINKING" TEAM GROWS STRONGER AND QUICKER TO RESPOND, LEADING TO LOTS OF DOWNSTAIRS BRAIN MOMENTS.[4] INSTEAD OF DEVELOPING A SUPER-SPEED ELEVATOR TO THE UPSTAIRS BRAIN, THE AMYGDALA STARTS WORKING EVEN HARDER![5]

REMEMBER...BRAINS CAN CHANGE![6] TAKE A DEEP BREATH, BE CURIOUS, AND CHOOSE TO THINK BEFORE ACTING. YOU ARE A VALUABLE BRAIN BUILDER.

If you are not sure that your cries and smiles mattered when you were little, this brain-building stuff might feel extra hard! You are not broken. Your child is not broken. There's HOPE.

Find books, free resources, and more support for the healing journey at www.JessicaSinarski.com.

[2] *The Power of Showing Up* (Siegel and Bryson)
[3] www.developingchild.harvard.edu
[4] *Riley the Brave* (Sinarski)
[5] *The Neurobiology of Attachment-Focused Therapy* (Baylin and Hughes)
[6] *What Happened to You?* (Perry and Winfrey)

TiPS FOR USiNG THiS BOOK AND BEYOND

Begin Using Brain-Based Language

Make it part of your classroom routine or family culture to check in with your brain. Show kids how you can talk to your Amygdala. Talk about Porcupine and Turtle moments—we all have them! Look for and celebrate Upstairs Brain moments too!

Get to Know Your Downstairs Brain Protectors

1. Think of a time you had one of these Downstairs Brain moments.

2. Where did you feel it in your body? What sensations or emotions did you notice?

3. What did you need in that moment?

4. What helps you keep your Upstairs Brain in charge?
   H.A.L.T. and check your basic needs first.
   We all struggle if we are Hungry, Angry, Lonely, or Tired.

Practice Telling the Whole Story

The brain is a story-making machine. When the Downstairs Brain is running the show, stories can get pretty negative toward ourselves and others. Try getting the Upstairs Brain involved! For example:

- "It makes sense that your Tiger Brain wanted to come out! Let's take some big deep breaths and figure out the rest of the story."

- "You were feeling really nervous. I bet your Amygdala was saying, 'Danger! Danger!' I see you decided to keep going. How are you feeling now?"

- My daughter has been having a Porcupine moment all afternoon!! My Turtle Brain wants to take over and run and hide. I am going to get a drink of water, text a friend who gets it, and turn on some music while I get dinner ready. Phew, I think I have enough lights on in my Upstairs Brain to be curious about why she is feeling so prickly today.

And remember, screens are no friend of the brain. Be sure to have lots of tech-free time with your kids!

Be a Safe Adult

The brain is quick to notice facial expression, tone of voice, and body language, so check in with yourself, especially in stressful situations. Relax your forehead, take a breath, and lead with your Upstairs Brain.

Keep Growing *Your* Amazing Brain

The brain-boosting tips in this book aren't just for kids! You need connection, movement, some broccoli, and a little playfulness in your life too!

If you work in the world of education, find some brain science to make your job easier at www.BraveBrains.com. And be sure to check out *Light Up the Learning Brain* for more brain-building strategies.

ACTiViTiES

What to Do When My Brain Feels Cluttered

When feelings get big, the staircase of your mind can get cluttered. Use your ABC plan to clear the stairs!

FRUSTRATED

EMBARRASSED

SAD

WORRIED

A Quick Pause

Try out these different ways to take a quick pause. Notice which ones work for you.

- Deep breath in, long breath out
- Shake it off
- Listen to music
- Pull out my journal
- Get a drink of water
- Talk to someone I trust
- Take a quick break

Be Curious

Our experiences and big feelings can feel like heavy books weighing us down.

Circle any books that are in your backpack today: Anger, Grief, Sadness, Frustration, Feeling Left Out, Hurt, Stress, Loneliness, Shame, Scared at Home, Feeling Powerless, Feeling Different, Embarrassment, Hunger, Guilt, Fear, Confusion, Rejection, Failure, Injustice, Jealous, Worried, Not Fair, Scared at School.

What danger is your Amygdala sensing?

Try putting it in a sentence:

I feel _____

when _____.

Choose Wisely

Time to clear the stairs and let your Upstairs Brain run the show. Choose one of these Bright Thought Bookmarks to set your heavy books aside or make up your own!

Visit **JessicaSinarski.com/Amazing** to download handout versions of these resources!

- It's okay, Amygdala, I've got this.
- I am not my feelings.
- I can do hard things.
- I am strong and courageous.
- Mistakes are part of learning.
- I can ask for what I need.

I AM THE BOSS OF MY BRAIN

I will practice these brain-boosting habits to strengthen my **THINK BEFORE ACTING** powers:

These are my Amygdala-calming strategies:

When my Downstairs Brain Protectors take over, I need:

GLOSSARY

Amygdala: Almond-shaped group of neurons in the limbic system that acts like an alarm and traffic director

Axon: Message sender in a neuron

Brain Stem: Quick-responding part of the brain in charge of automatic actions like breathing and heartbeat

Cells: Tiny working parts that make up your brain and body

Cerebral Cortex: Large, wrinkly outer portion of your brain that let's you connect, play, talk, learn, create, and think things through

Dendrites: Message receivers in a neuron

Downstairs Brain: Lower part of your brain made up of the brain stem and limbic system (aka the "act without thinking" team)

Glial cell / Glia: Brain cells that insulate, clean, feed, and support neurons

Limbic System: Feeling and memory center in the middle of your brain that colors sensory messages based on your experiences and emotions

Myelin Sheath: Message protector and accelerator in a neuron

Nerve: Bundle of axons that send information from your brain to your body and back to the brain

Nerve - Motor: Carries messages from your brain to your muscles

Nerve - Sensory: Carries messages from your senses to your brain

Nervous System: Network of connections between your body and brain

Neuron: Brain cell that sends and receives messages

Neurotransmitters: Little package of chemicals that neurons use to talk to each other

Nucleus: Instruction manual of a cell

Internal Organ: A part of your body under the skin that performs a specific function (i.e. heart, lungs, stomach)

Sense - Interoception: Information from the sensory nerves in your internal organs and skin that tells you if you are hot or cold, in pain or comfortable, hungry or full, etc.

Sense - Proprioception: Receiving information from your muscles and joints, this body sense helps you feel grounded and in control

Sense - Vestibular: This sense of movement and balance gives your brain little details from receptors in your inner ear to help you feel stable and anchored

Soma: The body of a cell

Spinal Cord: The highway through your spine that lets your brain communicate with the rest of your body

Synapse: Tiny action space between neurons where messages pass from one neuron to the next

Upstairs Brain: The upper, outer part of your brain made up of the cerebral cortex (aka the "think before acting" team)